Structured for Success: The 9-Point System to Create Breakthrough Business Results

Renaissance Works, Inc.
www.ren-works.com
success@ren-works.com

ISBN-13 978-0692204405
ISBN-10 0692204407

To business owners everywhere who work hard to provide for themselves, their families, and their futures, creating jobs for others and value for their customers. This book is dedicated to your noble contribution with hope that this will be a tool to make your work easier and your joy greater.

Acknowledgements

I express my heartfelt gratitude to the many mentors, friends, family, co-workers, and clients who have supported and encouraged me through my life. You have provided inspiration and encouragement that has helped shape the journey that I continue to be on – a future of possibility.

- To Keith, your generous encouragement and inspiration has helped me to grow my business owner skills over the years.
- To my Board of Directors, your ideas and encouragement have helped me to bottle my thoughts into this book.
- To Eric and Alicia, you have provided structures for my success.
- To Tony and Fred, who I miss greatly, you provided me opportunity and encouragement to grow my professional skills and confidence.
- To my mother and father, whose genes and dedicated parenting provided the pathway for me to learn and grow. Being the child of a star administrator and an engineer almost guaranteed I'd be structured!
- To O'Leary, your love, encouragement and support made this book possible.

Table of Contents

Foreword

Opportunity without structure is chaos. This one sentence summarizes the single biggest cause of frustration and exhaustion in the business world.

You have a great product or skill set which would be perfect for the market, so you decide to create a business around this idea. You always wanted to be your own boss, run your own business, call all the shots, set your own schedule and be in charge of your future financial rewards. But in the process of perfecting the product, finding the customers, and delivering the product or service to gain traction in the marketplace and produce revenue for your business, the back office, organization, processes and procedures stuff starts slipping through the cracks. The paperwork and piles on your desk grow daily. Customers become irritated with the lack of follow through or returned calls. Scheduling becomes spotty and delayed. Paying the bills gets relegated to some "To Do" list that now has 50 entries (or more likely there are 50 sticky notes with one "To Do" each because you can never seem to find the original master list). The billing starts to slip because there simply isn't time to do everything. Now cash starts to become an issue so the decision is made to simply work harder and longer to try to work your way out of the hole. Dumb!

Over the last forty-three years of starting, buying, selling, financing, restructuring and running businesses, I know first-hand the importance of leverage. In fact, leverage is the single greatest point of difference between owning a job and owning a business. Leverage means doing more with less. At the beginning, business owners are compensated for their time and effort. Sadly, there is a limit to the amount of time we have available and the amount of effort we can exert. Time and effort as a growth strategy result in revenues that are stunted and capped. No leverage, no growth. The result is chaos, confusion and a gravitational pull towards the urgent and not the important.

Business success requires business skills and tools. For the last fifteen years I have dedicated the majority of my time to teaching and training entrepreneurs in these required business skills and tools. In reality, I teach entrepreneurs how to build the bridge from business operator to business owner. A critical part of this transition is the leverage that comes with structure. Structure is the price business owners must pay for sustained business success.

I met Karen Logan in 2006 and have had the privilege of studying and guiding her every quarter of every year since. The knowledge and profound insights Karen has about business structure and the actionable steps required to create this sustainable success is in your hands. Karen has spent decades learning, practicing and perfecting her distinctions for *Structured Success*...and what she teaches works. She has an incredible track record of successfully advising, counseling and coaching business owners on the specific action steps required to breakthrough the artificial glass ceiling of exhaustion, frustration and chaos. Karen is one of those rare business experts who has learned it, done it, lived it and taught it to the small business community. If you study her experience and absorb her wisdom, you will be able to master these skill sets in days or weeks versus decades of trial and error.

The best thing about this book is what it will do for you after you read it. By taking action on the principles and tools Karen teaches, you will create the processes and procedures, design a blueprint, build an infrastructure and construct the systems that will return you to the thrill and passion of owning a business... and simultaneously allow you to grow your business and make more money.

Success is not an accident. Sustainable success requires leverage and one of the most critical forms of leverage available to a business owner is the leverage found in becoming *Structured for Success*.

--Keith J. Cunningham, author of *The Ultimate Blueprint for an Insanely Successful Business* and creator of CFO Scoreboard.

Introduction

Over the years, as I have talked with business owners who are colleagues and clients, I've discovered that most felt like their business was running them rather than the other way around. All of these people were creative and energetic, but each seemed to be missing the know-how needed to tame chaos. They found themselves with more work than they could handle, wrestling with a dilemma: "How can I fulfill demand and build a team when I am already overwhelmed?"

When I became a business owner, I began to realize and appreciate the joys and challenges that came with the job. I also noticed that my tendency to create structure allowed me to be organized in ways that some of my colleagues found magical. Being a natural teacher, I decided that writing a book featuring a step-by-step approach that would allow others to have this same success was a logical solution. It also provided a platform for me to think more deeply about some of the things that usually just come naturally to me.

This book is dedicated to helping you create a structure that will handle the chaos you may be experiencing now and position your business for growth into the future. This 9-Point System is your bridge from chaos to clarity and from overwhelm to order. Allow this to be your guide to more efficiency, effectiveness, and profit.

Some people feel overwhelmed when they think of the detail of their business. They don't know where to start in creating structure, plans, or strategies. Others feel that detail is not their strong point. Many of the people I have encountered are creative and free-spirited in their approach to work or business.

They like to follow their gut, emotion, or passion. For a while, these strategies may have served them well. But there comes a time when they need to look at structure and detail in order to grow the success that they have. Knowing and acting on the details of business can minimize lost revenues, wasted time, excess costs, errors, frustration, and stress. It can also buy back the freedom and creativity that you may have lost in running your business.

My commitment in writing this book is to make details clear, concise, and easy for you to implement. Pictures, models, and activities included in this book will allow you to immediately apply the learning directly to **your** business. My goal is to propel you toward increased efficiency and success by following the roadmap this book provides.

Best of success as you move forward with intention,

Karen Logan
President & CEO,
Renaissance Works, Inc.

Using Structured for Success

This book is designed to be solution-oriented. I invite you to use it as an opportunity to learn and apply the information presented to create a usable solution for more effectively and efficiently running your business. What you learn here is an opportunity for application in order to have the change you want. This book has been set up to help you create change and experience a breakthrough in your business. In addition to the content of each chapter, the components listed below have been included to help create distinctions and action steps to allow you to directly apply these concepts to your business:

1. **Structured for Success Stories**
   Be inspired by case examples from other business owners who have applied the tools in this book to create growth and productivity for their businesses.

2. **Structured for Success Examples**
   Learn distinctions and concepts from everyday structures that can be repurposed and applied to your business growth and productivity.

3. **Success Action**
   Engage simple questions and activities to help you build your **Structured for Success** solution.

4. **World Class Widgets**
   Gain access to templates, recordings, instructional articles, and other value-added tools that will allow you to apply the **Structured for Success** concepts introduced in the book.

Section 1.
Creating a *Structure for Success*

"Even if you are on the right track you will get run over
if you just sit there."
— Mark Twain

It is helpful to begin with the end in mind. That's how great businesses are built and sustained. Having a goal, objective, or outcome in mind will be helpful in making the lessons relevant and your decisions along the way clear and focused. Here are some outcomes you can expect as a result of completing this book:

- Articulate the value of structure for your business
- Identify the three main operational areas of your business
- Identify the three main productivity streams to optimize your business
- Identify and apply strategies to maximize your time, money, and resources
- Identify actions you can take to boost your productivity and profitability
- Create order in your current business

Best to you as you embark on your journey to be **Structured for Success**!

Chapter 1. Setting the Stage

*"Improved productivity means less
human sweat, not more."*
– Henry Ford

What is Your Story?

What's your story behind getting into the business world? Did you inherit the family business? Were you an "expert" at something and thought you would set up your own business? Did you get "downsized" and set out to reinvent yourself by starting your own business? Each of us has our own unique story, and yet we all share some common traits.

Many business owners were never taught how to run a business. They had skills for delivering their product or service and, if they're lucky, some natural gifts for sales or marketing. Unfortunately, most business owners experience tremendous gaps in getting their business to run orderly and efficiently. They lack the skills, tools, and systems that are needed.

As an example, one of our clients mentioned that he would regularly hit a "growth ceiling." He could only grow his staff to 6 – 8 people and it wouldn't grow any bigger. His problem, which many other business owners experience, was not having a structure in place to sustain growth. Once there were a set number of players on the team, it became too large for him to oversee without structure and systems in place to create order and clarity. In one of our strategy sessions, I was able to lay out a structure for his company that enabled him to see where the gaps were and how he could set himself up to create growth.

Immediately, he set out to start applying my 9-Point System to build the infrastructure needed to sustain the growth he desired. Now, his business is moving beyond his growth ceiling and thriving. He's even looking to apply this same approach as he begins to set up the business to franchise it.

This book has these 9-Point ideas packaged so that you can immediately apply them to your business for your own growth success. It's the "Structured for Success" recipe.

The Business Owner's Dilemma

Many business owners started small by providing a needed service or product based on their personal talent or expertise. You may have started this exact way. You may have started out by yourself or had a partner. As time went on and business became successful, you may have hired someone to help take on some tasks. Some business tasks were not in your skill set. Other tasks were not worth your time. You may have hired a bookkeeper to make sure the finances were taken care of. You may have outsourced a web designer to maintain your website because you didn't know how to do it yourself. But at some point, like most business owners, you reached your capacity to complete all the work that needed to be done. It was hard to keep all the "plates spinning!"

Here lies the business owner's dilemma: *How do you grow and become more productive when you are already too busy?* This dilemma is further compounded by the fact that most business owners were never taught how to run and grow their businesses. They are excellent at what they do, but lack the "knowhow" to get business done!

Yet you keep doing the best you can, throwing your best solutions at the problem. You think that if you get to work earlier or stay later or work weekends, you'll be able to catch up. You hire someone just to help and may find that the person is not right for the job. You may purchase a new gadget because it sounds like it will save time and you find out it is really more work and confusion.

These are symptoms that point to the problem of a lack of structure. This situation will remain, creating a growth ceiling, unless you change how you organize and relate to your company. Symptoms are warnings that something is not right. The problem will get worse if not solved. Just as our bodies provide warnings, that if left unheeded, can create bigger problems, so too, your businesses can provide warnings.

What will happen to your business if the pain is not addressed? Perhaps you are unaware of the cost of lacking structure and systems. You may have even forgotten what the joy of your work feels like, or what weekends look like.

Use this pain assessment tool to measure some of the warning signs of your business.

INSTRUCTIONS
1. For each typical business pain listed below, mark your pain level on a scale of 1 to 10 (10 being the most painful).
2. List the pain level number in the far right column.
3. Add the column scores.
4. Compare your total with the score metric to get a quick pulse of your businesses "pain" state.

Business Pains	Sliding Scale		Score
	Low	High	
1. Chaos/ Confusion	1 – 2 – 3 - 4 – 5 – 6 – 7 – 8 – 9 – 10		
2. Rework & Errors	1 – 2 – 3 - 4 – 5 – 6 – 7 – 8 – 9 – 10		
3. Long Working Hours	1 – 2 – 3 - 4 – 5 – 6 – 7 – 8 – 9 – 10		
4. Wasted Time	1 – 2 – 3 - 4 – 5 – 6 – 7 – 8 – 9 – 10		
5. Inefficient Processes	1 – 2 – 3 - 4 – 5 – 6 – 7 – 8 – 9 – 10		
6. Customers Lost Due to Team Incompetence	1 – 2 – 3 - 4 – 5 – 6 – 7 – 8 – 9 – 10		
7. Bad Hires	1 – 2 – 3 - 4 – 5 – 6 – 7 – 8 – 9 – 10		
8. Technology that Does Not Work	1 – 2 – 3 - 4 – 5 – 6 – 7 – 8 – 9 – 10		
9. Lost or Breached Data	1 – 2 – 3 - 4 – 5 – 6 – 7 – 8 – 9 – 10		
10. Frustration	1 – 2 – 3 - 4 – 5 – 6 – 7 – 8 – 9 – 10		
		Total Score:	

Scoring Levels:

0 – 20: Low pain but room for growth and improvement since there are always opportunities to gain more efficiency and effectiveness.

21 – 40: There is a lot that is managed and you're in a perfect position to refine and reduce the pain you have. Look for new discoveries and approaches you can apply to add more wins to your situation.

41 – 65: You've got some things handled but much opportunity for improvement. Take advantage of your progress to build more improvements.

66 – 84: Ouch! Things are coming to a boil and the pain level will move you and your team towards burnout. This book can help ease and remove some of this pain.

85 – 100: Yikes! Take comfort because you can begin to minimize your pain starting with the discoveries and actions you take from this book.

What new insights did you gain from this assessment of the symptoms? As humans, we have an amazing ability to deny, adapt, and overlook. We can live with chronic pain and not even realize that there is a cure or a level of relief.

> *!*
> "It is *now twice as hard to run a successful business* than it was a generation ago – Competitive intensity has doubled in the last 30 years."[1]

We may be completely unaware that we are in pain until the moment we discover pain relief and then a whole new world of freedom and joy is opened up for us.

Consider this a new window of opportunity to reclaim the joy or feeling of freedom you once knew in running your business. Take this as an opening to create more predictable and reliable results for the future you want to have. By taking on a learning mindset and applying even a few of these ideas, you can improve your situation and begin to be **Structured for Success**.

"If you could kick the person in the pants
responsible for most of your trouble,
you wouldn't sit for a month."
– Theodore Roosevelt

My Secret Discovery

In my early years in business, I worked for a small company. I got to see all the operations. Unfortunately, I also got to see how a company struggles and dies when it is not run effectively. This company made a best-in-class product, generating 2 million in  annual revenue but the owner did not run the business in a way that allowed it to grow and thrive. There were scattered systems in place to support the manufacturing efforts. However, there was no structure to handle the customer service, sales, and other key aspects of the business. When I was first hired, I was brought in to handle the "customer service problem." In a few short weeks, I put a system in place that categorized the incoming repairs, followed up on outgoing orders, and addressed the customer calls as they came in. Now there was structure! I not only got rid of the customers' headaches, but also my own.

The proof of the new system's effectiveness came in the form of the appreciation we received from our customers at our annual trade show. Our system made them look good to **their** customers. It was structure that created results – goodwill, increased sales, satisfied clients – all going to the bottom line.

Although this was a major improvement to the customer service, it was not enough to see the entire company successfully through to health. This was a business in need of a structure overhaul in a number of areas and in need of a business owner who was willing to lead the change. It was painful to be a part of a failing business, but as I look back, I see rich lessons that have helped me, as a business owner, help other business owners to keep their train from "going off the rails."

My next big business chapter was working for a major aerospace corporation. It was quite a change to go from a small business to a large corporation. At first, I felt like a small cog in the big machine. However, I quickly learned the cultural DNA that makes these large companies operate. Being naturally structured, I quickly absorbed the "bullet point" communications, the huge acronym vocabulary, and the systems that helped business flow.

I was fortunate to be working during the time that they were implementing world-class manufacturing principles. During these years I learned world-class efficiency and optimization techniques that were applied to create savings within the company. I eagerly volunteered to participate on special projects that allowed me to learn and apply these skills. It was rewarding to create value and to be recognized for making a difference in such a big organization.

Like most businesswomen with a dream, I eventually decided to start my own business, providing my expertise as a consultant to companies who were implementing a large software application called SAP. Now I became an "expert for hire" as well as a business owner, juggling the requirements of building systems to help large companies expand while also embedding the world-class systems I had learned into my own small business.

As I discussed experiences with other business owners, I realized I had unique tools that were helping me be successful and sustain growth. Those tools were from my big fortune 500, corporate upbringing and were naturally applied to my workday. My business owner colleagues were not familiar with them and were curious to know more. As I shared a few basic tools and templates, things started to click for them and a light bulb went off for me!

The more I worked with business owners, the more I found that these tools were creating huge breakthroughs in how owners thought of and approached their business operations. They began to see their businesses with distinct working groups. They learned how some of the tools and techniques created new clarity, order, and productivity for their businesses. It was helping business owners run their businesses and make the most of all of their resources, including their own time. These tools and approaches were helping others become structured for success. It was personally and professionally rewarding.

This book is the resulting natural expression of how I might help other business owners to be **Structured for Success** and to create their own clarity and sustained growth.

Chapter 2. What is Structure & How Does it Help Your Business?

"Form and Function should be One."
– Frank L. Wright

Structure provides stability, order, and clarity. Structure provides a framework so that specific actions and activities can be accomplished like winning a game or providing rescue services during a natural disaster. Structure can be represented by something physical, like a building, a bridge, or a sports team. Structure can also be found in more intangible things, such as reporting relationships, a process, or an agreement.

Structure is a critical component to a healthy, thriving business, and consequently, the importance of structure in business cannot be overstated. Most business owners see business structure as how they legally organized their company (e.g., LLC, S-Corporation, etc.). However, what I'm talking about here is putting in place a framework in which you can organize all the moving parts of your business into an effective system. This system ties together all the actions, activities, and people that are used to sell and deliver your product or service into an effectively running machine that is able to grow.

Unfortunately, most owners are unaware of the benefits of establishing structure in their business. Additionally, most owners have not been trained to identify and improve business structure. Instead, what most owners are keenly aware of is the worries that keep them up at night – those things that are not working in their business (e.g., problems with sales, production, quality, incorrect reporting, employees, complaints, and lack of revenue – just to name a few). I assert that implementing structure will solve many of your business "headaches" – or, at the very least, will make problems easier to identify and handle.

Structure in Our Everyday World as a Model for Winning in Business

> **Structure:**
> - (n.) A framework to have increased mobility, speed, accuracy.
> - (v.) Ability to create a sustainable and growing future.

Structure is everywhere. It provides stability and predictability. With it, you can know where you are and where you need to go. Just the simple table of contents of this book is structure. It's a roadmap and a high-level look at what is going to be covered throughout the pages. You have an idea of where you're going and it helps to make the learning easier. And structure can provide the same type of clarity in your business.

Looking at structure in what we experience everyday is a perfect place to see how it works and its value. We'll start with these basics as a model and then tie these ideas into working solutions for your business.

Consider various common physical structures:

- Human Body: A **body** has a **skeleton**
- High-Rise Building: A **high-rise** building has **steel framing**
- Bridge: A **bridge** has **cables, beams, pillars**

Each of these structures provides strength so that other elements (e.g., muscles, windows, roadway) can be added *without stressing the system*. Each of these structures *provides order* so that there is a logical flow and function to its pieces and parts, rather than collapsing into a twisted jumble.

Structured for Success: The Human Body

The human body is an amazing organism. In addition to its ability to heal itself, it has multiple abilities that rival those of many other animal species. The human body is able to work efficiently and effectively.

The body's structure is a skeleton, which has a couple of primary functions:

1. It provides a **framework** for connection points for muscles and tendons, enabling the body to move and perform actions.
2. It provides **protection** to the organs that enable the body to think, breathe, digest and perform other actions that sustain life.

Without the structure of the skeleton, the muscles, tissues and organs would be a formless blob and not be able to serve their purposes. Similarly, without the muscles, tissues and organs, the skeleton would not have the necessary elements to contribute value.

Structure is not an end in itself. It is a critical ingredient that provides for motion, growth, contribution, efficiency and protection. It's a necessary part of an integrated system.

Just as the skeleton is important in providing integrated structure for the operation of the body, structure is also critical for the mobility and operation of a business.

Without a structure, a business may be struggling to survive. It may be a jumbled collection of ideas and products and team members trying to figure out what they're doing, where they're going, and how they're going to get there without a framework to provide the direction. Structure provides the needed elements to create clarity, productivity and protection in order to move towards the goals and objectives of the business.

The structure of an organization has a purpose. Primarily, that purpose is to allow the other parts of the business to thrive.

Structure provides you a means to better organize all the "moving parts" in your business so that there is stability, order, efficiency, and effectiveness. A by-product of getting organized is the reduction of stress, uncertainty, and risk. This naturally generates a better experience of running your business and a better environment for you, your team, and your customers. Applying a higher level of order to your business will also make it much easier to manage, measure, and change, as needed. Oh, and by the way, you'll likely see positive results in your financial bottom line as you begin to implement these solutions, cutting waste (cost) and improving throughput (revenue).

In larger organizations, structure is set up to keep a large entity organized and running smoothly. They are more complex in nature, so breaking out the complexity helps to manage all the pieces and parts in, ideally, a more efficient way.

Smaller businesses typically start with no formal structure, usually with only one person, or possibly a few people, making up the entire team. It is the growing of the team and the increasing volume of

> "We can not solve our problems with the same level of thinking that created them." – A. Einstein

business that requires some form of structure in order to maintain order, direction, and efficiency. The mystery is in how to create a structure to grow when you may not have a roadmap. The 9-Point System described in this book provides the model and roadmap to use to move towards your business goals no matter the size of your business. From my experience, you've got to make it **simple** in order to make it **scalable**.

Where to Turn for Help

We often go to professionals when we don't know how to do something – how to balance our books, how to set up a website, how to get a patent. Sure, we could do it ourselves, but it might take a lot of time to figure it out, and even then it might not really be right. Hiring someone who knows how to do these things can speed up the process and increase the accuracy, professionalism, and efficiency of how these things get done. When you're first starting out, money may be a serious constraint and doing it yourself may be the most affordable answer. However, as you grow, you start to value your time in new ways and find that others can do things more affordably than you. This is the beginning of growth and leverage: to continually move towards the highest and best use of your time.

But how do you find a professional who can help you set up your business to run more effectively? So things run efficiently day-to-day? So you don't have fires to put out all the time? Who is the professional for that?

This book is the first place you can go to begin making your business effective, efficient, clear, and predictable. This book can provide you with a foundational structure that will better organize all the good things you have going in your business and unravel those things that have gotten tangled and confused.

Structured for Success: The Waste Wake-Up Equation

Lack of structure can waste incredible amounts of hard-earned cash. Without looking at the actual numbers, it's hard to determine what the lack of structure is actually costing you. It can start off as little bits here and there, but the truth is, it can add up very quickly. That is money being burned up!

Use this simple equation to calculate how much money you are losing with a lack of structure.

$$\textbf{(Wasted Time per Week) x (Weeks per Year) x}$$
$$\textbf{(Hourly Wage Rate)}$$
$$\textbf{= (Total Wasted Dollars per Year)}$$

Example:
Jill had a successful physical therapy practice. Jill had someone on staff who was in charge of billing the clients, but she found that she was regularly following up with reminders and double-checking this person's work in order to make sure it was done correctly. She was overworked and overwhelmed. Her cash flow was dwindling and her bills continued to mount. Something had to give.

We talked about her situation and created the following equation to understand how much money was being burned through the constant checking that was required.

Time wasted in double-checking someone's work:

Item	Amount
Time spent per week **finding out** if the billing had been done	12 minutes
Time spent per week **reviewing** billing statements to ensure they went out with the correct math	25 minutes
Time spent per week in addressing customer complaints about billing	30 minutes
Total minutes per week	67 minutes
Multiplied by 50 weeks per year (assuming vacation time)	1537 minutes (25.6 hours)
Multiplied by her billable rate (which might have been directed to billable work instead)	$125
Total Annual Amount of Waste	**$3,202.08**

I am sure that her estimates may have been lower than what was really happening. Many times we assess that something is taking only a few minutes, but as you can see, she spent a over a half a week per year following up on things that should have been completed by a competent person. As she thought of other time wasters, the number got much bigger – both in hours and dollars! It was a moment of discovery.

Considering all the many little items of waste, toleration, frustration, and error that can be encountered in a day, it's easy to see how profits can be eaten away and business owners can get burned-out.

Apply this equation to a simple task in your business that seems to be a "little" frustration and see how it is eating into your profits as well as your peace of mind.

In today's environment, successful business owners integrate and apply structure to maximize the productivity of people, processes, and technology. Great business leaders create the structure for business success in order to dynamically stay ahead of an ever-changing economy and business environment. It is a business truth that those who don't apply structure to win at the game of business will, unfortunately, be left behind.

Business is an endeavor that requires thinking and planning to keep ahead of the game! By reading this book and applying the thinking and practices we discuss, you will strengthen your business. Let's first set the stage with some of the basics of applying structure to your business.

World Class Widget
- Determine what time and money is being wasted in your business using the **Waste Calculation Template**. Go to: www.thestructuresolution.com

Chapter 3.
Putting Structure to Use in Your Business

*"You have to work hard to get your thinking clean
to make it simple."*
– Steve Jobs

Structures make activity easier, clearer, and in turn, more efficient and effective. That's what this book is all about – helping you create new kinds of structure in your business, while providing added *muscle* to move forward with focus, a *foundation* for higher levels of

productivity, and a *pathway* for people to have sharper and faster solutions.

Structured for Success: New Structure to Reach New Heights

Even as early as the Roman Empire, there were buildings as tall as five to seven stories, but the weight had to be supported by thick walls and the structures were not always stable. This thinking about buildings prevailed for centuries.

In the 1870s, high-rise buildings became possible with the use of steel beams for construction. From that point on, the use of steel combined with the invention of the elevator just a couple of decades earlier, created an ability to build towards the sky[1]. It has allowed populations to grow upwards, expanding living, business, and commerce, and creating economic advantages on a limited footprint of land. It has created efficiency and optimization of space.

The steel structure of a high-rise has a critical job of providing shape and strength to the building in order to hold up the weight and provide a framework for the other structural elements to be put into place.

If the building remained just a steel structure, there would be limited function or purpose. However, once the external "skin" and internal workings are added, there is possibility for life, productivity, and efficiency. Consider some of the unique elements of a high-rise building that is supported by its structure:

- Elevators for transporting
- Ducts and pipes providing key life elements of air and water
- Efficient use of a land footprint
- Views for unique perspective and value
- Single location for many businesses or residents

Similarly, the structure of a business will also create framework for productivity and possibility. Without a structure in place, people will try to figure out their work using their personal assumptions of how "it should be" and doing their best to fit in. That is a recipe for rework, frustration, and chaos.

What lessons can you take from the model of the high-rise? Where does your business currently stand in its use of structure? Most business owners have not really taken the time to get out of the day-to-day work to step back and assess where they stand. As my business mentor Keith Cunningham frequently encourages, business owners need to have regular "thinking time" in order to plan, assess, and dig into where they are, what the real problems are, and what the best solutions might be. I have found that carving out consistent thinking time has helped me to elevate out of the day-to-day activities and begin to create better perspective on my situation. Thinking time is an underutilized structure element.

Let's elevate the conversation and take some time to assess your current structure situation.

Assessing Your Current Structure Situation

Knowing where to start is the first step to getting where you want to be. How to create a bridge across your business gap is part of what you will be able to learn through this book. But first, it is helpful to know your starting point.

Use the assessment below to identify the level of structure you currently have in place in your business.

1. For each structure tool listed below, circle the score that best reflects your current situation.
2. Add the individual column scores.
3. Add all column scores together.
4. Compare with the score metric to get a quick pulse of your business' "structure" state.

Structure Tool	Yikes, do I need this?	On my "to do" list.	Hmm, somewhat	Pretty much done.	All up-to-date!
1. Organization Chart (Org Chart) by Functions	1	2	3	4	5
2. Process Flow Charts	1	2	3	4	5
3. Written Job Procedures	1	2	3	4	5
4. Marketing & Sales Scripts	1	2	3	4	5
5. Meeting Agenda Template	1	2	3	4	5
6. Employee Handbook	1	2	3	4	5
7. Sales "Plan vs. Actual" Report	1	2	3	4	5
8. Trend Analysis for Budget vs. Actual Costs	1	2	3	4	5
9. Technology Back-up Processes	1	2	3	4	5
10. Employee Job Expectations	1	2	3	4	5
Column Scores:					

Total Score (sum all columns): _____
Scoring Levels:

10 - 20: Playing with fire!
21 – 30: Shooting from the hip.
31 – 44: Scratching the surface.
45 – 50: Taking the bull by the horns.

How did you score? Like most business owners, there is probably room for improvement. However, the big discovery is considering how much money is left on the table or flat-out wasted by not having these structure tools in place. (By the way, these are just a few key structure tools that successful businesses need.)

Think of the chaos in your workplace because people don't know how to complete tasks correctly. How much wasted time and depleted morale occurs because there are aimless meetings where little or nothing is accomplished? What risk exposure do you have without a technology plan to back-up and secure financial, customer, inventory, and other data? A lost file, an employee who leaves, or a customer who doesn't come back, all hit the bottom line of your business' profitability. However, by putting even a little structure in place, you can begin to minimize waste, chaos, and confusion, while maximizing productivity and profit.

Let's begin to set the stage for your new and winning world by starting to build structure for your business.

Chapter 4. Laying Out a Structure to Win

"The only place where Success
comes before Work is in the dictionary."
– Vince Lombardi

As a business owner, you may wear many hats to keep your business running. These hats represent the different responsibilities and functions that are required to make business happen: making customers happy, keeping bills paid, and maintaining operational throughput, to name a few. How many hats do you wear? If you're wearing most (or all) of the hats in your business, you may feel ready to lose the head that those hats are covering!

One way to look at business structure is by seeing how your company's activity is organized. Is your business broken into small functional teams? Is it organized around products that you create? Are your teams grouped around taking care of daily circumstances? Perhaps there is not a distinct order. It may feel like a group of people doing a "bunch of stuff" and "things just happen" in order to "keep up."

To bring clarity and structure to your business, you need to break out the overall business into distinct and understandable pieces. I'll call this "chunking it down." This is a place where we can take a lesson from big corporations. They have to be organized because there are so many people and so many things that need to get done. They have an approach that breaks down the large company into departments, for example, in order to better group and manage the workforce and their responsibilities. Big companies may have an accounting department, a manufacturing department, a sales department, a legal department, and so on. They may have a number of people in each department and these people all have a particular assignment, function, goals, tasks, and responsibilities.

There is an advantage to breaking out your business into distinct and understandable pieces, regardless of your business size. In this way, you can manage the "machinery" of your business, and it becomes easier to understand and simpler to change and improve. Creating simplicity in the midst of busyness and demands will help give you peace of mind and provide a pathway for you to move towards running your business, rather than your business running you.

Structured for Success: The Department Store

We can learn from so many structures outside of our business paradigm. The department store, for example, is a common structure that allows us to go to one location and find a number of different items. In 1878, a *New York Times* headline announced, "The Great Sixth-Avenue Bazaar; Opening Day at Macy & Co.'s – A Place Where Almost

Anything May Be Bought." The special attraction, the article noted, was the "universality of the stock, almost every article of dress and household furniture being for sale there, and at the most reasonable prices."[1]

The distinct feature of the department store is that everything has been arranged to better service the customers. Like items can be found grouped together. There is usually a directory that tells people where everything is located, and clerks are ideally hired with the expertise required to answer customer questions for those areas. There is order and support that makes the store function for the customer.

From the business' perspective, there is economy of scale for the administration and advertising, and this can allow for lower prices and better marketing leverage. There is order and leverage for the business.

It is a time-tested model that we have even seen move to the Internet. This "department" approach will be seen when we go to Amazon, eBay, or other online retailers. Like items are grouped to help the customer better search and find what they want to research, compare, review, and buy.

The idea of departments can apply to small and mid-sized businesses as well. For example, the concept of similar products, revenue streams, functions, and processes being grouped together can then allow for

> **!**
> ● *"94% of business leaders say planning ways to manage the complexity* is critical to their company's success."[2]

similar skills, temperaments, and other resources to be better leveraged.

Let's look at how we can apply the department store concept to your business.

Breaking Business into the Basics

Take a typical small to medium-sized business. Its high-level functions typically break out into three main functional components:

- **Marketing & Sales**
- **Operations**
- **Back Office**

In large companies these three areas might be called departments or divisions. For our purposes, I will call them functional areas, but they all represent the same concept – breaking the business down into logical groupings. Regardless, whether it is a Fortune 500 company or a garage start-up, every business has at least these three distinct functional areas.

These three areas, Marketing & Sales, Operations, and Back Office, can be expressed by the main activities that are completed in these functional areas: selling, producing (goods and/or services) and making sure all the paperwork and finances get taken care of. More simply, I call these three areas "Sell It", "Do It," and "Care for It".

As a business owner, viewing your company through the lens of these three high-level and basic functions already makes things clearer. This perspective helps you to partition your thinking and strategizing. You can break your problem-solving and idea-generation down into these groupings in order to focus on the specific needs of each of these areas. This perspective allows you to specifically address the staffing, processing, and technology needs that are required for each of these three areas.

If you think of your business as one big entity, with hundreds of actions to complete and decisions to make, it becomes an overwhelming proposition and is an inefficient approach – like putting all your problems into a blender and hitting the purée button.

Breaking your activities into these distinct functional areas allows you to organize your business into a meaningful structure. This structure will enable better strategic thinking and better decision-making. You will be able to put on one "hat" at a time and consider what is needed to make that area more productive or less prone to errors.

Basic Business Building Blocks

These three basic areas or departments set up the first basic building blocks that will be used for the 9-Point System. Each of these areas has its own particular focus for contributing to a thriving, productive business. Knowing the focus of each area helps you to identify outcomes and influences decisions that are specific to those areas.

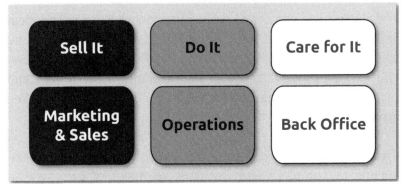

Figure 4.1 Basic Business Buildling Blocks

Marketing & Sales: "Sell It"

This part of the business is primarily **externally focused**. That external focus is to the marketplace: current and potential customers. There is a need to let the marketplace become aware of your business through marketing activities. Plus, there is a need to support your customer in their desire to solve their problem through your sales activities.

The "Sell It" area has a mission, objectives, outcomes, and activities that set it apart from the other areas in your business. It also will require specific personalities, skills, technology and problem solving to help it thrive. Because of these unique needs, looking at the "Sell It" area apart from the other areas will provide you the opportunity for thinking about how to best address these needs. You will be able to wear this one hat and consider the decisions and activities that will be required to make this area function well.

Operations: "Do It"

This part of the business is also primarily **externally focused**. That external focus is to the customer. Activity in this area provides the creation and delivery of the final product and/or service. It also provides support to both new and existing customers, such as warranty repairs, customer service, or helpdesk support.

The "Do It" area also has its own mission, objectives, outcomes, and activities that set it apart. It requires specific personalities, skills, technology and problem solving to help it thrive. Looking at this one area apart from the others enables you to consider the decisions and activities that will be required to make this area function effectively.

Back Office: "Care for It"

This part of the business is primarily **internally focused**. The internal focus is to the employees, data, compliance, and other elements that ensure that the business can continue to operate. Activities in this area include making sure that the health of the business is measured and maintained through documenting finances, legal compliance, data integrity, as well as other measures and transactions. This area supports the other two areas so they can perform their distinct focus.

The "Care It" area, too, has its own mission, objectives, outcomes, and activities that set it apart from the other two. It requires its own specific personalities, skills, technology and problem solving to address its unique needs. Addressing those needs apart from the other areas will provide you with the option to focus and consider the decisions and activities that will be needed to make this area function as it should.

All three of these areas have a special focus that is critical to effective overall success and general well-being of the business.

Breaking out your business activities into these three functional areas simplifies thinking for you as a business owner. At any given time, you can ask yourself or your team, "What area are your current actions supporting? How effective are your actions in supporting the focus of this area? What percentage of my time is spread across each area?" In the case of one person who wears many hats in your business, the identification of what area you are supporting can be more directly connected with the focus and outcomes of that area. In short, this first layer of structure already begins to organize your business and thinking in a way that can support your decisions and actions to boost productivity and reduce headaches!

Success Action Steps:

1. What **functional area** do you see your personal daily business activity fitting into?

2. Which **functional area** do you think you have the most understanding of?

3. Which **functional area** may be missing, neglected, or under-represented in your business?

4. In which **functional area** does your skills and abilities best fit?

Chapter 5.
The Winning Trio for Geting Business Done

*"Order and simplification are the first steps toward
the mastery of a subject."*
— Thomas Mann

In the last section, we broke your business into three functional areas to **organize your business**. This created a foundation on which to build the 9-Point System. The next building blocks will be the key elements that are used to **get business done**. The three elements are **people, process,** and **technology.**

- **People:** The *team* who gets the job done
- **Processes:** The *way* things get done
- **Technology:** The *tools* to get it done faster, better, more accurately

These are elements that you have working in your business today. The distinction here is to create a structured way to think about these elements that will ensure they are addressed and work together as a winning trio to get business done.

People

People are **the minds, hands, feet, and voices that get things done** in your business. They are the most important part of this three-part structure. People can make your business shine and be highly profitable, or they can make it dysfunctional and full of errors and "oopses". People (your team) connect with your customers. They represent your brand, they interact with other team members, they think of new ideas. They help you make money. They make the sales, build the product, deliver the service, and pay the bills. They may also resist change, create havoc, make errors, or steal from your inventory.

> ❗ *Most businesses incur an average of 4x the hiring salary when hiring and training a new person.*[1] *If you don't hire the right person and set them up for success, you may find yourself spending this amount multiple times in a year.*

When we talk of people, we are referring to anyone who helps your business get the job done. This may be employees, vendors, contractors, temps or other external service providers. They all influence your branding and productivity.

Whoever is a part of delivering your internal or external products and services is a part of your team and should be considered as part of the overall functional structure of your business. Figure 5.1 shows the variety of possible team members a business owner has as options for getting business done.

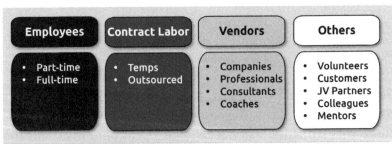

Figure 5.1 Business Team Members

Additionally, all team members, whether employees or not, should be considered in the overall branding, expectations, and interconnection of your business. All team members need to be considered a part of your business machine. Effective teams will have good communication, appreciation, clear expectations, and accountability. Whether a team member is an employee or an outside vendor, the overall success of your business relies on an effectively led and managed team.

Who can affect or change your bottom line? Anyone who "touches" your business has the power to impact you whether it's an employee, a vendor, or a disgruntled customer on Yelp. For a savvy business, realizing the full scope of your team can help you create a broader strategy than you may have originally considered, leveraging unexpected and underutilized resources.

Structured for Success: Eliminating the Single Point of Failure

Sometimes the "people" in our business is only the business owner. With small teams, there may be only one person filling a key role. When there is a situation like this, you are looking at a "single point of failure." This is a term that comes from the technology world, used to describe how a system can fail through the breakdown of one of the links in the chain.

In the case of your team, there is possibility of a broken link in the chain of the process when only one person has the knowledge and skills to complete a key task in the business. If that person becomes sick or leaves the business, essential knowledge or functionality is lost. This can affect productivity, revenues and even remaining "open for business."

This is huge risk for business owners and one that should be identified with a plan for putting a "safety net" in place so that the risk can be mitigated. By looking at this expanded view of a team, an unrecognized resource may be added or cross-trained to strengthen the chain and eliminate the single point of failure.

A business cannot function without people. People moving together in the same, productive direction will create maximum revenue and a thriving future. This happens with effective integration of people, processes, and technology. Being aware of all the people who make your business happen is a first step towards moving into more productivity.

World Class Widget
- Find the value of having a structured approach to on-boarding and growing your team by accessing the infographic **Life-Cycle of a Winning Team Member**. Go to: www.thestructuresolution.com

Processes

> *"Even the best, most motivated people in a broken process will create subpar performance."*
> *– Edward Deming.*

Processes are *the story of how things get done*. Every process is a recurring event that has a beginning, a middle, and hopefully, a happy end! Every task or activity that's required in your company, such as paying bills, answering the phone or assembling a widget has a process associated with it. There is usually a logical flow and a linear aspect to each process. There may be some twists and turns if there are errors or exceptions, but usually there's a step-by-step method to getting the job done.

Unfortunately, in most businesses, the process is left to chance and experimentation. Most people carry the details of how things are done in their heads, using assumptions and their best estimates to complete daily activity or to address unexpected circumstances. Some people on the team will

> *! "98% of businesses do not have their processes written out."* How much would your company loose if the best person who "knows how it's done" *leaves the team* with all that knowledge in their head!

do it one way, while others do it another. Without written processes or expectations, a team member who might come into work one day in a sad, angry, or impatient mood will most probably complete tasks differently than the day they come in with a happy, hopeful, or excited mood. This haphazard approach will create "lumpy" results, errors, and customer confusion. That will impact the brand of your business and may cause you to lose customers. Inevitably, this situation creates waste and leaves additional fires to put out. Without written processes and the discipline of your people following them, repeatable success can feel like trying to win the lottery.

The antidote to unpredictability is to have written processes. Written processes that can be used for training, creating expectations, and improving productivity are essential. Writing things down establishes a reference source and a baseline to create clarity and capture improvements. It can also help mitigate single points of failure.

Written processes can be as simple as checklists or step-by-step instructions. The information can be visualized and organized into picture flow charts or tables. The key is to get it "on paper" so it can become a part of the working success of your business.

The successful integration of motivated, trained **people** with sound, repeated **processes** is a key to good performance. Good people and good processes are a winning combination. But wait, there's more!

Technology

Technology represents **the tools used to get business done productively.** Technology includes computers, hardware, software, the Internet, social media, cell phones, mobile devices, and scheduling tools. Technology can obviously include these "high-tech" items (e.g., the latest electronic devices or applications) but it can also refer to "low-tech" solutions (e.g., ergonomic chairs, white boards, or lighting), which can also increase productivity.

> **!** "80% of the software implemented *does not provide the expected return on investment?* And over 60% of these implementations *go over budget!"* [2] This could drain profits and efficiency, costing you many times the amount of the initial software.

Technology is everywhere in our culture. It's shiny and "cool". We feel pressure from advertisers and peers who insist that some app or gadget is the greatest thing and we've got to have it. However, implementing the latest technology is not always the most efficient, nor the most effective solution. "Old school" methods, such as paper and pencil, may be the most effective solution for sketching out a quick diagram, especially if the person does not have a software tool on which they are proficient. A simple phone call to a customer may be more effective in sales than "IM-ing" (instant messaging) them the latest company product. What is critical as a business owner is to determine what technology will save and/or create money, and which ones will eat up money and not provide a payback.

Structured for Success Story: Avoiding "Tech Regret"

I spoke at a technical event recently, where I performed a short survey for the attendees about applications they had on their mobile phones. Most people had over 100. They were also asked, of these apps:

- How many apps are productive? (Average: 12 of 100)
- How many apps are time wasters? (Average: 15 of 100)
- How many apps are not used? (Average: 80 of 100)

As you can see by the results represented in this survey, just regarding phone applications, all that glitters does not produce gold!

Taking this to the business workplace, the complexity increases. There are so many options available for software, online applications, desktops, laptops, mobile devices and more. Many people think that if they get the latest software package or start using an online solution, it will be the answer to all their problems. However, just purchasing a new product isn't a solution. There is much more to consider when introducing any technology into your business.

Software or online applications are typically unforgiving and very demanding. They require specific inputs and rigid, disciplined processes in order to perform effectively. They demand regular upkeep and upgrades. They require predictable processes, uniformity, and many decisions for setup. They need people to be adequately trained to use it properly and require disciplined use in order to provide meaningful service.

Hardware also requires a number of decisions in order to have the appropriate speed, space, security, user-friendliness and integration with existing technology.

There are many considerations before making the financial investment to implement technology. First and foremost:

1. What problem are you trying to solve?
2. Is this the best way to solve it?

Prior to engaging a software or technology project, it is wise to do a lot of homework, understanding your desired outcomes and talking to others who have already implemented similar solutions. A salesperson will say it does everything. On the other hand, a business owner will let you know what they wish they had asked ahead of time. All too frequently, you learn the software can "do everything" but it costs extra to buy the "added package" or customize it for that task. In addition, the training included to use the new software is often not enough to get your team sufficiently ready to go.

The best way to avoid "tech regret" is to do the necessary thinking, planning and research to ensure your investment will provide the return you are seeking.

Technology should operate as a contributing "team member," providing reliable and stable 24-hour service (e.g., ecommerce, website, on-demand videos). If leveraged correctly, technology can allow business to happen while you sleep. It can be a big time saver and a reliable "keeper and reporter" of data. As a business owner, you want to utilize all the options that provide the most efficient and cost effective solutions.

Be keenly aware of how you will leverage technology. Implementing new technology is usually disruptive to productivity at first. Lost time is irreplaceable. Not all team members or customers accept or can learn about new technology at the same rate. Your team may be adverse to technology, so implementing the latest, greatest technology is never going to be a good solution for them. User adoption rates and usage of technology varies between generations. It is key to consider the integration of your people with your technology when making a technology decision. We will explore technology deeper as we move into the 9-Point System in more detail.

Success Action Steps:

1. On a scale of 1 to 10 (10 high) how would you rate the efficiency of your people (team)?

2. On a scale of 1 to 10 (10 high) how would you rate the effectiveness of your processes?

3. Which three technologies in your business contribute to producing the most revenue or reducing the most expenses?

4. Which technologies are draining time and money?

World Class Widget
- Find out other tips on avoiding "tech regret" by accessing the article **Avoiding Tech Regret**. Go to: www.thestructuresolution.com

Section 2.
Applying the 9-Point System

"We shape our buildings; thereafter they shape us."
— Winston Churchill

Now you have been introduced to the basic building materials for the 9-Point System:

- 3 areas for organizing your business
- 3 elements for executing your business

The 9-Point System is a 3-by-3 structure that will allow you to systematically approach your business to make it more efficient and effective while providing a model for you to make better decisions. To build out this 3-by-3 structure, each **functional area** will have its own **people**, **processes**, and **technology** requirements. The 9-Point System is illustrated in this diagram:

Marketing & Sales (Sell It)	Operations (Do It)	Back Office (Care for It)
1. People	4. People	7. People
2. Process	5. Process	8. Process
3. Technology	6. Technology	9. Technology

Through this simple structure, you will be able to get your business finely tuned and positioned for growth and tability. You will be able to make better decisions about spending money, hiring people, outsourcing, and engaging technology.   No matter how many people, processes, or technologies you have, you will be able to leverage this model from your starting place and use it as a tool to grow. This is a business structure that is flexible and scalable.

This section of the book will walk through this 9-Point System, providing ways to optimize and integrate each of these points into your business. Successful companies leverage each of these 9-Points to become more profitable and productive. Dismissing, omitting, or ignoring one or more of these 9-Points will likely create a sinkhole for money. Integrating this 9-Point System will create a highly efficient and effective business "machine."

As we look at each point, you will be able to put on one "hat" at a time and elevate your thinking.   As a business owner you will be able to create a strategic action plan to implement these ideas into your business. This step-by-step process will greatly help you as a business owner to break out all the moving parts into manageable components and make it much easier for you to think about growth for your business.

You will see this icon (shown on the next page) as representation of the 9-Point System throughout the book. Each chapter in this section will use this icon as a roadmap, showing which point is being discussed.

9-Point Icon

Consider how this 9-Point System can help you solve problems, create order, and implement immediate adjustments. Be sure to take the time to do the activities and check out the resources so that by the end of the book you will have completed your own **Structured for Success** solution.

Chapter 6.
Point 1: Marketing & Sales -- People

"If opportunity doesn't knock, build a door."
– Milton Berle

The 9-Point System begins with the people who support the "Sell It" area. This is the group of people who will let the marketplace know you are in business and ready to make a sale. They will nurture the current customers and invest in new customers. In a way, they kick off the process of getting business through the pipeline.

The types of skills and personalities that thrive in this area may not excel in the Operations or Back Office areas of your business. By considering this first point of the 9-Point System, you will already begin to carve out specific distinctions that can help you improve your hiring, leading, and management over this area.

This team will drive the processes of marketing and sales. Think of these people as those who will take on the job functions required for the "Sell It" area. Here is a list of some typical job functions found in this area:

- Sales Representatives: those who will sell the product
- Web Developer: those who will update the website

- Public Relations (PR) Representative: those who will handle getting your name out to publications and social media
- Advertising Team: those who drive product campaigns
- Copywriter: those who will create compelling stories and descriptions
- Marketing Agent: those who will be responsible for your presence in the marketplace
- Account Rep: those who will take care of your current customers and previous customers
- Event Coordinator: those who will set up and coordinate events (speaking, training, social, networking, etc.) targeted to your market

You may have all, a few, or just one of these job functions currently in your business. You may also have additional roles that are appropriate for your type of business. You may personally fill all of these roles or have other people that are responsible for them. Whatever your situation, clearly identifying and defining the needed roles or job functions is a key part of creating your business success structure and having a clear idea about the people required to best execute the tasks this area needs to thrive.

Even if you fill all these roles for now (e.g., you wear all the hats), as you continue to grow your company and develop your business, you will eventually decide to have someone else fill some of the roles. Part of growing your business means replicating your skills and

> **!**
> • "75% of employees are frustrated because *they don't always know what to do or what is expected of them?"* Think of how establishing clear roles, responsibilities, and expectations could make your company *go from fuzzy to fantastic!*

expertise through others, so that you're available to take on larger challenges. For example, if you are currently doing web development, you may later decide that you are unable, or that it's impractical for you, to continue filling this role. You may conclude that it is now time to have a reliable and technically capable person take over this task, in order to free you up for larger responsibilities, and to make better use of your time and skills. Through this process of identifying these job functions, you have created an expectation for this role to exist. When it's time to delegate the role you will be ready to move into action and hire, outsource, or move the function to another person within your company.

Structured for Success Story: Crisis Averted, Weekend Discovered!

James is a high-energy and very successful salesman. In the past seven years, through a challenging economy, he had almost singlehandedly led a social media team to generate $2 million in gross annual sales. James now wanted to double the double the net cash flow and to be able to hire more people in order to free up some time for his much-needed weekends. He didn't really know where to start since he felt tired and overwhelmed.

I found out that he was responsible for more than 80% of the sales and decisions for his business. He had 12 employees but still struggled to delegate effectively. He was charismatic, quick-thinking, and hard-working.

We listed out the functions required for his team and noted which roles each team member took on. In the current layout for his "Sell It" team, there was a major issue pending – he was the only one taking on any selling activity. All new leads were channeled through him. In other words was a "single point of failure" for this critical funnel for his business. If something happened to him, there would be no one else trained or prepared to take on the selling tasks and the company would soon run out of new business.

We approached the "single point of failure" and the "weary business owner" challenges by coming from two different directions asking these questions:

1. How might you replicate what you're doing through others?
2. What activities are you doing now that are not the most productive and best use of your time?

First, we created a way to replicate his selling skills through a "ride along" program with two of his team members who were currently working in the Operations area and showed some natural abilities in sales. Using a transition plan of partial time in Sales and partial time in Operations, these two would fully transition in a 6-month period, providing additional cash flow and training time to find and bring on new people to take on their old duties.

Second, he listed 20 tasks, each that were consuming small bits of time throughout the month but added up to about 25% of his total activities. These were low-level activities that he was willing to delegate. Team members were identified to take on these tasks along with the requirements, deadlines, and standards of quality required. He would transition these tasks over a 30-day period.

James immediately felt a weight off his shoulders. He saw that the changes were obvious and possible – he just hadn't made time to look at his organization this way and see how to better allocate the resources he had. He was so busy in the trenches that he hadn't elevated his perspective enough to see the lay of the land. By delegating the small tasks, he built trust with his team. He also saw amazing results from the two members that were taking on the sales activities.

The transition plan created a new environment for the team, too. People really stepped up as they saw that they could make a contribution to the company's success in bigger ways. They saw James taking on the leadership that they were hungering for and sales and net cash started moving up immediately.

If you understand the functions required for your business to run you will have more clarity to determine your gaps, overlaps, and single points of failure. What might you find as you look at the "Sell it" part of your business?

Success Action Point 1:

- List the **People** (job functions, team roles) needed to get the **Sell It** (marketing and sales) part of your business accomplished.

Marketing People (functions/roles)	Sales People (functions/roles)
1.	1.
2.	2.
3.	3.
4.	4.
5.	5.

World Class Widget

- Access the "**Sell It" Team Functional Worksheet** to capture the **People** needed for your Marketing and Sales area. Go to: www.thestructuresolution.com

Chapter 7.
Point 2: Marketing & Sales -- Processes

"You don't close a sale; you open a relationship if you want to build a long-term, successful enterprise."
— Patricia Fripp

Your business has certain marketing and sales activities that are taking place or should be taking place. To create sustainable growth there should be marketing and sales processes that are written and used. This is where the magic of checklists, step-by-step procedures, and scripts is captured and used.

The processes and activities that are a part of marketing might include email, hard-mail, and social media campaigns. These activities might be replicated on a weekly or monthly cycle. Each *type* of marketing effort would have a unique individual process which would have step-by-step instructions, dates of activities, trigger points, and standards.

The typical processes and activities for marketing and sales might include:

- Creating a sales campaign
- Making a sales call
- Following up on a warm lead
- Launching an email marketing campaign
- Updating social media posts

- Creating the weekly newsletter
- Setting up a new customer
- Preparing for a weekly sale meeting

These processes should be written down in the form of scripts, checklists, or procedures. They are all meant to secure and nurture customers and future revenue commitments in a consistent way, using the best practices that reflect your company's branding.

Structured for Success Story: Discovering the "Sell It" Process Gap

I was working with my client John, who was a business owner and managing partner at his accounting firm. The word-of-mouth referrals from their long-time customers was working pretty well, keeping the business going and growing at a nominal rate. However, his firm had in place a long and complicated process that had to occur before a referral could be brought on as a client. This created a huge lag in revenue and cash flow. Although the firm was trusted and beloved, the process that was needed to move a business from "interested" to "being served" was holding up the level of growth that the business owner desired.

I worked with John and introduced him to the concept of the 3 functional areas. His "ah-ha moment" was seeing he had no formal Marketing and Sales area! It was all him in that department, and he was overworked and overloaded, which created a bottleneck for a staff that was ready to take on more clients.

By carving out the "Sell It" area, we were able to talk strategically about his current marketing and sales activities and identify options to create better flow and efficiency. It further opened the fear that he had about marketing and sales, which is common amongst many business owners who are excellent at delivering their product or service.

John was able to determine the next steps because of his new awareness. He also gained confidence that he could grow and not be overwhelmed for the future.

By taking his business and breaking out the functional areas, it was much easier to analyze and address the sales situation.

Listing out the marketing and sales activities that you are already exercising, along with ones you would like to include, is a critical part of creating a structure to build on. This inventory of the "Sell It" processes allows you to see what you have and begin to identify what is missing or needed. The great news is that you may be able to fill some of those gaps with resources found on the Internet, in classes, in pre-packaged programs or through the expertise of a team member you currently have on staff. Take a first step by creating the list!

Success Action Point 2:

- List the **Processes** (activities, actions) needed to get the **Sell It** (marketing and sales) part of your business accomplished.

Marketing Processes	Sales Processes
1.	1.
2.	2.
3.	3.
4.	4.
5.	5.

World Class Widget

- Access the "**Sell It**" **Processes Worksheet** to capture the **Processes** needed for your Marketing and Sales area. Go to: www.thestructuresolution.com

Chapter 8.
Point 3: Marketing & Sales -- Technology

"The spirit must prevail over technology."
– Albert Einstein

Technology can be a powerful tool for handling your marketing and sales area. With technology being a key communication medium, there are many options available from traditional to new media. Integration of new technology can be complex, expensive, and yield spotty results. In the "Sell It" area, it is critical to weigh the cost versus benefit option when making a business decision. It is all too easy to be wooed by the hype and feel like you might be the last person "to the party". Stand firm to make a calculated decision so that you don't create chaos and overwhelm yourself and your team.

Consider this list of technology options you might use as part of your "Sell It" area:

- Website
- Social Media Presence
- Mobile Devices
- Communication Devices
- Computer and Software Technologies
- Customer Relationship Management (CRM) System
- ecommerce Tools (e.g., shopping carts, payment systems)

- Email systems for marketing

Technology should be selected on the basis that it makes business easier for you, your team, and your customer. Part of your evaluation of integrating technology is deciding if the investment of time and money will create more sales, more customers, and greater productivity. If not, then a simpler process solution may be in order. For example, you may want to answer phone calls personally instead of using an automated

> **!**
>
> ● "*The cost to get a new customer is 2 to 4 times more expensive than selling to an existing customer?*" Consider how many of your customers are lost daily because of unfriendly or incompetent service. Your team is your front line. They should be trained and prepared to provide consistent, excellent and repeatable service to your customers.

system. Keeping the answering "in house" may provide the strategic advantage that allows you to create a personal relationship with your customers that converts into higher sales, loyalty, and satisfaction. You may decide that using Facebook for business is not something you have the resources for, or it may not be where your target market is. You may determine it is a strategy to employ later if you are setting up other marketing avenues.

Sometimes "low-tech" solutions may be effective, such as using a clipboard with a checklist or table on a printed page for salespersons to capture how the client found out about your business, instead of having the customer enter their response into an iPad or respond to an email survey. Decisions are made by carving out thinking time to ask questions that dig for meaningful answers. I credit one of my mentors, Keith Cunningham, for this equation that helps us to make a better fact-based decision given this question: How much time and how many resources will provide what type of return in what timeframe? I have interpreted Keith's equation into the diagram provided here.

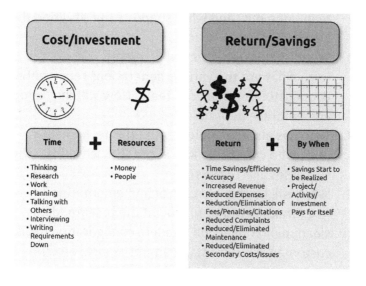

Figure 8.1 Return on Investment Equation

This equation works well in situations where emotions may take over. Certainly, it is appropriate in the area of technology decisions when a lot of money can be quickly spent on something that may just "be cool."

Consider these questions when adding technology:

1. What problem are you trying to solve?
   (Being specific here will help you select the best solution and verify that you are not selecting something just because it glitters and is cool!)
2. What is your Geographical Diversity?
   (e.g., do you have a remote team, an on-site work team, or a mix, and what supports the situation the best?)
3. What is your Generational Diversity?
   (e.g., what are the various generations represented by your customers and your team. How will they adopt and embrace it, or not?)
4. Who has already implemented this technology?
   (e.g., who can you talk to in order to learn from their successes and regrets?)
5. What will be the real cost of implementation?
   (e.g., training required, downtime to learn, data cleanup or conversion needed, configuration decisions, customer adjustments, team resistance, etc.?)

Structured for Success Story: Growing Pains Solved

Frequently we see people who are outgrowing their current solutions, but they are so used to their processes that they have not realized they need a new solution. This was the case for the Michaels. They were a husband-and-wife team who owned a growing training company. They used a free email communication system for their regular marketing messages and used a spreadsheet to keep track of their prospects, leads, and customers. They were in the process of figuring out how to use an online shopping cart when they went into "technical overload" and contacted me to discuss their problem.

As I talked with the Michaels, I could see that they had a clear vision for growing their business. They were just not sure how far they were going to get with their current tools, lack of technical skills, and limited budget. We explored their current team members and found out that they had recently lost their administrative assistant. We discussed specific solutions and leveraged the equation (Figure 8.1) to determine "how much time and resources were needed to get how much return and by when."

The final solution was to move to single online CRM (customer relationship management) system. This tool allowed them to eliminate the email system and the spreadsheet database. With this CRM tool, they would have those two items and the shopping cart all in one system. They hesitated to say yes because of the monthly fee associated with the tool. However, the fee was only a fraction of the monthly salary they had paid their administrative assistant who had been in charge of updating both of the older, more cumbersome tools. Also, they would be gaining automated reporting from the system which had been completed manually. It would cost less in the short term to go with the shopping cart package, but in the long run, they would have needed to migrate data, learn a new system, and still live with the inefficiencies of the current system.

They decided that a one-time change for a system that they may take a little time to grow into was still the best choice. After making the decision, they found that it also motivated them to play into that bigger game – an interesting side effect! In addition, many of the tasks manually performed by their admin were now automated. The trade-off in "who" performed the task created an immediate cost savings of $500/month. The ROI was quickly captured and the new revenue opportunities were increased substantially.

You may feel some growing pains with the current technology that you are using. Be sure that you evaluate your decision to upgrade or add new technology carefully. It is all too easy to be seduced by a salesperson who is not familiar with the needs and limitations of your people, your process, and your budget.

Success Action Point 3:
- List the **Technology** (high- and low-tech options) needed to get the **Sell It** (marketing and sales) part of your business accomplished.

Marketing Technology	Sales Technology
1.	1.
2.	2.
3.	3.
4.	4.
5.	5.

World Class Widget
- Access the **"Sell It" Technology Worksheet** to capture the **Technology** needed for your Marketing and Sales area. Go to: www.thestructuresolution.com

Chapter 9.
Point 4: Operations -- People

> *"The most unprofitable item ever*
> *manufactured is an excuse."*
> *— John Mason*

Next, we move into the **Operations** area, starting with the People or job functions that are typically seen in this part of the business.   Where Point 1 of the grid welcomed in the customers, Point 4 provides the goods and services for the customers, continuing the process of moving business through the pipeline.

The types of skills and personalities that provide value in this area may be quite different than the "Sell it" or "Care for It" areas. The skills and experience here are specific to your type of business. If you run a smaller business, or are the main expert for your business, this may be one of the areas where you hold off hiring additional team members. Conversely, if you know this part of the business very well, you may be able to hire more successfully to replicate the skills that you know well.

Your team members are the *people* who will make up the Operations area.   As I work with various businesses, I find that it helps to break the Operations area into subcategories that represent the revenue streams or products or services that are provided by the company.

To better illustrate, I will use an example business: a carpet cleaning company. This business has three distinct revenue streams with a support team who helps get the business done. The three revenue streams are:

> **!**
> • *"At any given time 54% of employees are not engaged in work. Even* among the best performers, only 35% said they are working at their full potential."[1]

1. Carpet Cleaning*: Commercial Properties
2. Carpet Cleaning*: Residential Properties
3. Water Restoration Services

* Also includes tile, grout, vent cleaning, and other services.

The decision to partition the business into these 3 revenue streams had to do with the types of people (skills, personalities, temperament, etc.) that were unique to each of these services. **Commercial** accounts were typically serviced after-hours with empty rooms. The service person went in and did his job, then moved to the next room. There was no requirement to interact with a customer, provide additional service or sales support, or have an engaging personality. The hours were also in the evenings. On the other hand, the **Residential** service person needed to be well-mannered and may have needed to perform sales tasks while in the customers' homes. The **Water Restoration Services** required individuals who could be on-call, and these individuals needed to be trained and certified appropriately. Finally, there was a group of people who needed to take the call, order the supplies, and perform other activities that supported all three of the revenue streams.

The benefit in breaking out the operational areas into sub-groups is that it allows you to consider more options and learn how to make more informed hiring, compensation, expectation, and management decisions.

Summary Look at the "Do It" People for the Carpet Cleaning Business:

- Carpet Cleaning: Commercial Properties
  - Commercial Technicians: those who will clean carpets, tile, grout, ducts for commercial properties (restaurants, vacant apartments, retail businesses)
- Carpet Cleaning: Residential Properties
  - Residential Technicians: those who will clean carpets, furniture, tile, grout, ducts for homeowners
- Water Restoration Services
  - Water Technicians: those who will clean up water issues and work on the restoration processes
- Operations Support Team:
  - Shop Foreman: someone who will manage the shop, the team, and the equipment. Makes sure that reports, invoices, and timecards are processed and forwarded to the Back Office. Ensures that regulatory requirements are followed and that certifications are up-to-date.
  - Customer Service Representatives: those who will support customer questions, complaints, and remediation
  - Dispatcher/Scheduler: someone who will take incoming customer calls, create the daily schedule and dispatch the technicians

- Trainer: someone who will provide the training or obtain training for team based on certification schedules and requirements of the business
- Buyer: someone who will purchase required supplies and equipment

Structured for Success Story: The Revelation of Undiscovered Resources!

I worked with a small carpet cleaning business that was run by a husband-wife team, Jeff and Stacey. They were both smart and dedicated people but were struggling with the difficulty of getting everything done, even with a team of workers to support them.

We sat down at their dining room table and started brainstorming the job functions (people) that they needed to support their operation. We took sticky notes and began listing one job function on each individual note, and then organized them on the table. We filled in sticky notes for the "Sell It," "Do It," and "Care For It" areas. We completed a half-table of sticky notes! It was fun, easy, and most importantly, it elevated the conversation from day-to-day firefighting into **who do we need to get things done**.

As we looked at each sticky, we then assigned the names to the job functions – who was doing what. We then asked, "Is that the right person to do the job?" There were a number of sticky notes with "TBD" in the Sales and Marketing area. Cash flow was low. Stacey mentioned her frustration in not being able to find the right person to support the sales activities and she was constantly tied up in the Back Office with the books and paperwork. Since she had a sales background, we determined that it would be easier to transition her current bookkeeping tasks to another person and move her into the Marketing and Sales area. She had already set up processes and systems that would allow her to train a new person.

By taking a look at the business structure for People, we were able to begin to create a plan for efficiency, effectiveness, and for growth. We determined how many weeks it would take to be financially ready to bring on that person, wrote out the job expectations, and began a search for the right candidate.

They have since implemented the plan and are creating new results with their marketing tactics, building their referral base, and creating new sales and relationships that were readily available due to their long-time connection with their community.

As you consider your business, note which of these job functions fit your business model and determine how you will break your Operations area into sub-groups. Which roles do you need to add that you hadn't thought of before? Create a placeholder for each of the roles you think will support your business now and into the future (perhaps 12 – 18 months). This will provide you with room to grow your business, and your team members will also have room to grow in their career paths.

Success Action Point 4:

- List the **People** (job functions, team roles) needed to get the **Do It** (products and/or services) part of your business accomplished. Think of setting up sub-groups by revenue stream or product.

Sub-Group 1 People (functions)	Sub-Group 2 People (functions)
1.	1.
2.	2.
3.	3.
4.	4.
5.	5.
Sub-Group 3 People (functions)	**Sub-Group 4 People (functions)**
1.	1.
2.	2.
3.	3.
4.	4.
5.	5.

World Class Widget

- Access the "**Do It**" **Team Functional Worksheet** to capture the **People** needed for your Operations area. Go to: www.thestructuresolution.com

Chapter 10.
Point 5: Operations -- Processes

"Give me six hours to chop down a tree and I will spend the first four sharpening the axe."
— Abraham Lincoln

The Operations ("Do It") area is usually where most business owners had their start. It may be the area that you know best and could potentially be a blind spot for finding growth opportunities, efficiency, or looking to leverage other resources to accomplish the tasks. This area includes the creation, delivery, and support of your products and/or services. Support processes might include activities like customer service and inventory management, which support the production activities.

When you begin to list the processes that are required to deliver your products and services, you set the stage to create more clarity about what needs to be accomplished in order to group tasks, reassign tasks, outsource, eliminate, or streamline tasks.

> **!**
> • *Hit-or-miss processes lead to hit-or-miss performance.* "Companies with systematic processes to guide employees are 250% more likely to outperform competitors."[1]

Part of the power of applying the 9-Point System is grouping, sorting, listing, and discovering. Writing things down makes it visual, and when it is visual, it can be organized and discussed with others. Just a simple list of the processes you complete in your operations can engage your team to say, "I didn't know we did that," or "Don't we also do this?"

This list then can be the beginning of your inventory of everything it takes to get your product or service completed. From this point, you can begin to mark off what you have written down—whether in steps, a form, or a checklist—and what still needs to be documented. This exercise is a quick way to begin assembling your business' operational manuals.

The incredible power of writing things down is that you no longer need to have it stored in your head. If you are indeed the expert of your business, capturing your steps, thinking, analysis, and processes on paper or electronic media means that you have created new opportunities for growth. You have now created an asset for your business and are able to train someone else to replicate your style, quality and skills. You have also freed yourself for other things.

The other powerful aspect of writing things down is in minimizing the pain of lost knowledge. If you have key players on your team who do things better than anyone else OR who have knowledge that no one else has and its not written down, you are at risk to lose that forever if they leave your team. Have your team write their "recipe" down and start forming your company manuals. The manuals can then be used to enable your business to grow.

Continuing with our sample carpet cleaning business, the list below represents processes associated with some of the job functions we listed in the People section. Note how each job function will have a number of processes associated with the outcomes related to their position.

- Carpet Technician
    - Prepare van for service runs
    - Provide carpet cleaning service
    - Complete quality check for carpet cleaning
    - Complete daily paperwork
    - Clean van at end-of-day
- Customer Service Team
    - Complete follow-up for service call
    - Resolve a customer complaint
    - Conduct client visits
- Shop Foreman
    - Conduct daily team meetings
    - Complete end-of-day paperwork/invoices
    - Set-up weekly tech schedule
    - Manage van service and repair
    - Discipline/coach team members

If we looked closely at the Service processes in more detail, we would have recorded activities such as: how to clean various types of carpets, how to interact with the customers, how to complete and submit the bill to Accounts Receivable, and so forth. These processes would have step-by-step instructions, due dates, timeframes, and standards required so that quality and timeliness were reflected.

This list of processes may be used for other similar businesses such as plumbing, air conditioning, or electrical businesses. For other business types, create a list that would support the activities that directly service the customers or create the products. The main goal is to create clarity by writing down the list of activities that are part of delivering the products and/or services that your business provides.

Structured for Success Story: Investing in Future Security

Jeff, a prominent personal trainer, approached our company to help his business get some of their processes written down. Of particular concern was the 5-day workshop they provide to other personal trainers in order to certify them in their unique approach. He said, "If my general manager leaves or becomes ill, I don't know the details of what he does and I will be dead in the water." I worked with his team to determine the end-to-end process for delivering the workshop.

I took the General Manager and the support staff through an interview process, asking them questions about how a student signs up for the course, how they pay, how they get confirmation, and so on. We went through the entire process, asking "what happens after that" about 40 times until we reached the end of the process. During the conversation, it was reassuring to see that the General Manager was very organized and had a pretty well thought out process. It made it easy to write it down. However, there were a number of things that the business owner/instructor was taking on that could be easily delegated to some of the other training support team. The activity of getting all the expertise in one room, writing down the process, and having a conversation about the overall flow was illuminating to all. We found that there were missing documents and forms, there were openings to automate certain steps through their CRM system, and there were opportunities to train up other team members to take on more tasks and make a greater contribution.

The written process was used as a working checklist for the upcoming training. It has continued to provide a backbone to their operations for this one process. Additionally, it continues to be adjusted and updated as they think of more improvements and add new team members.

Jeff no longer worries about losing the knowledge of his General Manager and has enjoyed the increased freedom to develop new trainings and new team members through the activity of capturing this key process.

Listing the processes your business performs is the first step in creating security for your future. The loss of a key person can create chaos and risk for your business. Writing things down is an investment for your future.

Success Action Point 5:

- List the **Processes** (activities, actions) needed to get the **Do It** (product and/or service) part of your business accomplished. Leverage the sub-groups that you had set up earlier.

Sub-Group 1 Processes (activities)	Sub-Group 2 Processes (activities)
1.	1.
2.	2.
3.	3.
4.	4.
5.	5.
Sub-Group 3 Processes (activities)	**Sub-Group 4 Processes (activities)**
1.	1.
2.	2.
3.	3.
4.	4.
5.	5.

World Class Widget

- Access the "**Do It**" **Processes Worksheet** to capture the **Processes** needed for your Operations area.
  Go to: www.thestructuresolution.com

Chapter 11.
Point 6: Operations -- Technology

*"It's suppose to be automatic, but actually
you have push this button."*
– John Brunner

Technology can be a big timesaver and revenue generator for your Operations area. In the following list, you can see some of the options that are often a part of the service and product delivery:

- Dispatch Software
- Mobile Devices
- GPS System
- CAD Software
- Inventory Tracking
- Point of Sale System
- Scanners
- Phones
- Computers
- Plotters, Printers
- Automated Assembly Line

"62% of business owners say that determining how to best analyze existing information to improve decision-making is a critical goal they're falling short of." [1]

Technology should be selected if it makes business easier for you, your team, and your customer. Often automation can improve throughput, reduce errors, and allow team members to work on higher-level tasks. Being clear on the outcome desired from the use of technology will be critical for making it pay off. The return on investment will need to be balanced against both the obvious and hidden costs of implementation.

Structured for Success Story: The True Measure of a Win

Technology can be daunting, especially if you don't consider yourself to be a "techie." One of our clients was looking at her end-to-end process when we began to explore ways for her to allow prospects to take on more of the "information gathering" process. Belinda had a consulting firm that helped businesses regain their compliance certifications and get their companies back on track.

Belinda's process was to perform an assessment of the business through a 60 – 90 minute interview and then spend 2 – 3 hours in analysis and estimating for the project. Many of the businesses that would come to her were not serious about correcting their problems and did not engage her services. So all these hours spent were unbillable and were increasing the overhead costs of the business. Further, prospects were not really invested in the process, so it was easy for them to spend minimal time and walk away.

Through our discussion, we explored the possibility of gathering this upfront information with some automation in order to relieve the company of some of the risk and to engage the prospect in a more accountable way. Since Belinda was inexperienced with technology, we opted to create a solution that would test if the process could work in a "low-tech" method before pursuing other options. We designed a simple questionnaire that would be submitted prior to an appointment being set. We further created a checklist the project manager could complete prior to providing a package to the business owner. All these steps were created to simulate a potential online form and delegate some of the lower-level tasks to others who were building their skills.

This low-tech process is still in place because it was a successful solution that gave a quick win for a cumbersome and expensive process.

It cannot be overstated enough that integrating technology requires careful consideration. Be sure to engage a trusted and experienced person to help you think through your decisions. Trying out your "technical solution" in a manual way is an effective method for testing to see if the process steps are even going to help your business.

Success Action Point 6:

- List the **Technology** (high- and low-tech options) needed to get the **Do It** (product and/or service) part of your business accomplished.

Sub-Group 1 Technology	Sub-Group 2 Technology
1.	1.
2.	2.
3.	3.
4.	4.
5.	5.
Sub-Group 3 Technology	**Sub-Group 4 Technology**
1.	1.
2.	2.
3.	3.
4.	4.
5.	5.

World Class Widget

- Access the "**Do It**" **Technology Worksheet** to capture the **Technology** needed for your Operations area. Go to: www.thestructuresolution.com

Chapter 12.
Point 7: Back Office -- People

Finally we move into the **Back Office** or the "Care for It" area. As you think about your Back Office, there may be functions you never have thought of as being a part of your business. Remember that the Back Office focuses primarily on *internal* aspects of the business: supporting the team, and reporting on the health of the business overall. Where team members for Point 1 (Sell It) welcomed business and Point 4 (Do It) produced the business, Point 7 (Care for It) provides the needed support to keep the business flowing through the pipeline by billing customers and paying the team, to name a couple of key activities.

In many small and mid-sized businesses, the activities that are a part of the Back Office area may be outsourced and most times are not on site during daily operations. However, the working definition of your team is

> **!**
> In the 1950s the government decided to do the **first ever audit** of a new industry called aerospace.
>
> They went to the tycoon inventor, Howard Hughes, who only gave them 5 minutes of his time.
>
> The auditors asked, **"How many people work for you?"** Howard slowly leaned back in his chair and said, "About 50%."

all the players that make your business happen. Including the outsourced services as part of your team make-up prepares you to be proactive about decisions, management, leadership, and accountability. As you operate in this extended definition of your team, you can ensure that branding, quality, and communications reach these key players as well.

Because this part of the business is responsible for ensuring the safety, compliance, data security, financial integrity, and overall health and wellbeing of the business, this area is a critical one to inventory and staff. The breakout of this area would include these high-level areas with the associated job functions:

1. **Financial**: bookkeeping, accounts receivable, accounts payable, banking, etc.
2. **Technical** (IT): desktop support, back-up and upgrades for computers, software and applications
3. **Human Resources** (HR): employee on-boarding, benefits support, scheduling
4. **Payroll/Timekeeping**: payroll processing, payroll taxes, timecards
5. **Office Management**: purchasing of supplies, addressing office equipment issues
6. **Facilities**: taking care of the housekeeping and maintenance of the office, plant, or building
7. **Legal**: patents, counsel, trademarking, insurance
8. **Compliance**: ensuring the employee certifications or business permits are up-to-date

You may notice by the diversity of topics listed that there would be an associated diversity of skills and abilities required.

Most business owners are not skilled at many of the job functions required for this area and sometimes are quite overwhelmed by even thinking about them. Too often business owners will defer to other professionals because they believe these professionals should know better than they do. Unfortunately, owners may completely release responsibility for tasks to others, letting the activities get out of sight and out of mind. Be clear that delegation and abdication are two distinct approaches to getting business done[1]. Abdication creates a dangerous pathway to theft, misunderstanding, and increased costs. It also keeps you from gaining knowledge and using other's expertise to help inform your business decisions.

Delegation, on the other hand, is about responsibly transitioning a task to an individual who has the ability to complete the task and has been provided the proper expectations and instruction in order to be successful.

When job functions are outsourced to a professional, it is critical to ensure that these individuals are clear on their responsibilities and provide you with regular "easy to understand" reports. This is particularly true when these tasks are not in your area of expertise. Make sure that you understand what services they are performing and press back with questions until you feel comfortable with answers provided.

There are many opportunities for you to diversify your team based on your budget and your requirements. Vendors and contract labor may be a good fit if you do not have full-time work or you do not have a specific skill within your company. Alternatively, you may choose to have a fully staffed team of employees, creating many cross-training opportunities in order to have coverage if there are seasonal peaks in your business. Your requirements and constraints will provide the framework for how to best structure this team – for both the immediate and long-term timeframes.

Structured for Success Story: The Case of the Unexpected Asset

One of our clients, Beverly, leveraged an online jobs site to post a job for a transcriber. She found a candidate that met her needs and delivered the requested work on time and accurately.

The transcriber mentioned that she was excited about what Beverly was doing and jotted back a note of support. During that same time, I had been discussing this idea of defining Beverly's team more broadly to include those who are not necessarily employees. Even these individuals are resources that can be cultivated for more leverage. Beverly mentioned the unexpected response of the transcriber and decided to pursue a dialogue with her about her other skills, interests, and abilities.

Beverly found that this person understood her business and hired her to do some complex writing for a new project she had just taken on. Using this resource to work on this project increased her profit margin and allowed her to work on obtaining further contracts.

By expanding her definition of team and pursuing a simple opening, she was able to outsource some of her work, multiplying her capacity and creating a new option for saying yes to other business.

Success Action Point 7:

- List the **People** (job functions, team roles) needed to get the **Care for It** (back office) part of your business accomplished.

Back Office People (functions)	Back Office People (functions)
1.	1.
2.	2.
3.	3.
4.	4.
5.	5.

World Class Widget

- Access the **"Care for It" Team Functional Worksheet** to capture the **People** needed for your Back Office area. Go to: www.thestructuresolution.com

Chapter 13.
Point 8: Back Office -- Processes

"We often miss opportunity because it's dressed in overalls and looks like work."
— Thomas Edison

When you start to write down the **Back Office** processes that are needed for your business, it's helpful to list them out in the various subgroups that are applicable to your business. The underlying impact of structure is taking something that is large, complex, chaotic, or complicated and reducing it to smaller and more understandable pieces and patterns.

> **!** *"53% of employees don't have a clear understanding* of how they contribute to their company's goals."[1] *An effective plan would create processes that vividly communicate expectation and success criteria...*without hard-to-manage bureaucracy.

The **processes** in the **"Care for It"** area cover the following sample items, which are similar in most industries:

- Financial:
  - o Processing invoices
  - o Collecting on delinquent accounts
  - o Processing insurance payments

- o Running month-end reporting
  - o Reconciling bank statements
- Technical (IT):
  - o Backing up files
  - o Upgrading software
  - o Troubleshooting network issues
- Human Resources (HR):
  - o Posting a job opening
  - o Onboarding a new hire
  - o Processing drug and background checks
  - o Processing health insurance sign-up
  - o Filing employee paperwork
- Payroll/Timekeeping:
  - o Collecting timecards
  - o Submitting timesheets for processing
  - o Processing weekly payroll
- Office Management
  - o Ordering supplies
  - o Maintaining office copier

If we looked closer in the Finance processes, we would have step-by-step instructions on how to process a bill from a vendor or how to make a bank deposit, and so on. For our discussion here, we are laying a basic foundation of the processes that would be a part of your inventory for your company manuals.

Structured for Success Story: The Miracle of the Manual

A retail pharmacy wanted to create manuals to cover all the processes that were covered by retail and back office areas. It was a fascinating project, to learn the operations for filling prescriptions, ensuring quality and maintaining inventory tracking compliance. When the project was completed, the 3 main teams (Pharmacy Services, Retail Services, and Back Office) each had a manual with all the unique processes, checklists, and forms required to run each department. There was also an employee handbook so everyone knew the "rules of the road" when they came to be a part of the team.

Within a few weeks of completion of the project, the Office Manager, who had previously taken care of all the back office tasks, left the company without any notice. She had been a part of the team for many years. She knew many of the customers, all of the doctors who had accounts, and the various idiosyncrasies of the billing software. She had been the single source for employee paperwork when they were hired and helped to get everyone set up with various benefits. She was responsible for a huge set of tasks, and now she was gone without warning.

The Pharmacy Manager quickly designated one of the Pharmacy Techs to take the open position. The Tech had been particularly involved with the management of the logistics of drug orders. She was really good with the software and had an interest in building her skills and career in the company.

As good fortune would have it, the manuals were a major reference source. Since all the HR and Finance processes, checklists, and forms had been documented, there was a fresh and reliable source of information to provide a self-study crash course on how to run the Back Office. Without these manuals, all the steps, requirements, passwords, phone numbers, due dates, and contact names would have been lost or jumbled in miscellaneous files and sticky notes. This company would have potentially incurred fees for late payments, missed taxes or lost revenue on accounts receivables. The proactive approach of this business owner to create operations manuals provided tremendous savings in this critical area.

A number of sensitive and critical processes take place in your Back Office. Even if you have outsourced these tasks to trusted and long-term professionals, there may be a time when they are unable to serve your business. Make sure that you have a list of key tasks they perform for you, who their contacts are, and copies of key documents. If you need to transition the tasks or reply to an audit, you will have information you can fall back on.

Success Action Point 8:

- List the **Processes** (activities, actions) needed to get the **Care for It** (back office) part of your business accomplished. Leverage these sub-groups of activities:

Back Office Processes (Finance)	Back Office Processes (HR)
1.	1.
2.	2.
3.	3.
4.	4.
5.	5.
Back Office Processes (Regulatory)	**Back Office Processes (Other)**
1.	1.
2.	2.
3.	3.
4.	4.
5.	5.

World Class Widget

- Access the **"Care for It" Processes Worksheet** to capture the **Processes** needed for your Back Office area. Go to: www.thestructuresolution.com

Chapter 14.
Point 9: Back Office -- Technology

"We are stuck with technology when what we really want is just stuff that works."
– Douglas Adams

Technology can be a critical contributor to your **Back Office** team. Just as in our other areas, a careful look at what problem needs to be solved is essential. In the "Care for It" area, there is usually a lot of sensitive information. It needs to be stored in a way that is accurate, secure, and complies with applicable regulations (e.g., HIPAA, etc.) Any technology solution would need to provide for appropriate security and back-up so data is not lost or does not find its way into the wrong hands.

Here is an example of some possible Back Office technology:

- Accounting Software or "cloudware" (which may be an application or package that includes sales and information data as well)
- Phone system (this may be VOIP, traditional land lines, cell phones, or a combination of these)
- Computers (including laptops, desktops, and mobile devices)
- Online sales taxes processing
- Online timecard or payroll processing

Technology for the Back Office may need to integrate with other areas of your business. For example, the sales, production, or inventory information, which all have financial components, may be more efficient or accurate if

> **!** "40% of turnover is due to unnecessary job stress." [1]
> Technology can give management visibility into process breakdown or inefficiencies that create that stress.

they are part of the whole package. Applications that include a billing function, for example, may also capture related financial data. If there is a sales application that does not effectively integrate with the accounting application, there may be extra and wasted effort to do double data entry. The two applications may provide different sets of data that may make it harder for you as a business owner to make the needed decisions. The financial implications for your business make it all the more important to:

- Understand the various functions of your business
- Make a careful assessment before deciding to purchase new technology

However, with the thinking and discovery you have begun to take on through reading this book, you are much further along the learning curve than most business owners! This is only the beginning of the thought process, and a wise business owner will engage a number of people to help in making decisions about purchasing software, applications, hardware, or other technology.

Structured for Success Story: Simple Tech for Better Financial Health

Eileen has an online marketing company and has thousands of people following her and participating in a multi-tier training system. Each of the 4 tiers provides access to more content at a higher membership rate. She asked our team to help put in systems and document her processes so that she could grow her business. She was already aware, through our prior conversations, that she had some gaps in having things written down and had seen the value in getting some help to get it completed.

On our first meeting, it was easy to see that Eileen had tremendous skills in marketing and sales. As we began working with her we discovered that there were many "leaks" in tracking her financial results. She had an overall feeling that a lot of sales were being made and there was money in the bank, but she was unable to answer some basic questions about her overall business health. The financial part of the business baffled her. She thought all she needed was for the bookkeeper to keep track of the ins and outs and that the tax guy would make sure the taxes were paid.

We started by talking to her about the relationship of sales with revenues. She indicated that tiers 2 and 3 were her top revenue generating clients. My partner asked, "How do you know that?" She answered, "Well, I know that we get a lot of people signed up for those weekly." I followed up, "Do you ever get a report that shows how much revenue for each tier per week?" Eileen answered, "No, I don't. But that would be great!"

We proceeded to work with her to put together a financial dashboard – a one-page tool that would keep her updated weekly with some of the key financial measures needed to help her to see the health of sales, revenues, and cash flow. It would also show what expenses were due and what payments were delinquent. In our conversation, we found out that there was other information that would help her figure out if she would have enough cash in the bank to make payroll or upcoming bills. And the beauty of it was that tool was a simple spreadsheet that would be updated and presented weekly by her bookkeeper. Eileen didn't have to put it together or figure it out. She just needed to review it, ask questions, and provide direction that the bookkeeper could address and then report back.

In just a simple conversation, we were able to create awareness of a gap and figure out a very simple technology that could support the current volume of the business and be easily populated from data that was already being collected in various places in the company.

Eileen felt surprisingly empowered and was amazed to learn that financial reports don't have to be complicated. Yes, there are more complex reports, but our goal was to get Eileen engaged in the money management of her company so that she could keep a finger on the financial pulse of the business.

One of my favorite adages is: "What gets measured, gets managed[2]." When you begin to measure, you begin to become aware. With awareness comes the opportunity to change, and if there is change, then you can have something better than what you have now.

Eileen started measuring her basic financial activities and became aware of the ebb and flow of cash, sign-ups, expenses, and more. She was able to make better decisions on how to change her sales strategies and refund policies to better manage the overall health of her company.

Where might you put in simple technology to make your understanding of the health of your business more clear? Technology solutions in the Back Office should only be selected if they help the business owner ensure that the business has the cash, compliance, and security to keep running. In this area, more than most, the need for careful and complete recordkeeping is a critical function for the on-going care of the business, customers, and employees.

Success Action Point 9:

- List the **Technology** (high and low-tech options) needed to get the **Care for It** (back office) part of your business accomplished.

Back Office Technology (Finance)	Back Office Technology (HR)
1.	1.
2.	2.
3.	3.
4.	4.
5.	5.
Back Office Technology (Reg'tory)	**Back Office Technology (Other)**
1.	1.
2.	2.
3.	3.
4.	4.
5.	5.

World Class Widget

- Access the **"Care for It" Technology Worksheet** to capture the **Technology** needed for your Back Office area. Go to: www.thestructuresolution.com

Section 3. Putting It All Together

"Some are born great, others achieve greatness."
– Shakespeare

Congratulations on the work and thought you have put in so far. You have laid the foundation to be **Structured for Success** by learning and applying the 9-Point System. This unique 3-by-3 model allows you to look at the:

- 3 ways to organize your business
  - Sell It, Do It, Care for It
- 3 ways to get things done in your business
  - People, Processes, and Technology

Each of these 9-Points are bite-sized pieces that allow you to strategically think, plan, budget, hire, and make decisions that are more focused and directed towards your overall business goals.

This 3-by-3 grid is the first step in getting your business **Structured for Success** so that it can be organized, thrive, and grow. As a business owner, you now have the new option of putting on "one hat at a time" and of breaking out all the moving parts into manageable components.

Chapter 15.
The 9-Point System in Your Business

*"It's the job that's never started as takes
longest to finish."*
– J.R.R. Tolkien

The 9-Point System is meant to provide you, as a business owner, an approach that will allow you to understand and manage your business. Breaking your business into these distinct components has provided a means of elevating your thinking about the people, processes, and technology that you may have or that may be needed in order to support each of these 9-Points. You now have structure to identify gaps, overlaps, and risks.

However, to have a successfully running organization, the 9-Points are designed to be integrated into a well-coordinated "machine" -- each area working cooperatively and connected to generate smooth, daily activities.

Structured for Success: An Orchestra

Structure provides stability, order, and clarity. Structure provides a framework so that specific actions and activities can be accomplished. New ideas about structure can be learned by looking at the successful structures of other organizations.

An orchestra, for example, is an amazing organization that creates beautiful music at the seemingly mysterious waving of a conductor's arms. It may look like a bunch of people sitting in a group, all focused on the conductor. A closer and more educated look would show that there is a structure in place that creates order and supports the effective functioning of the group.

The diagram below (Figure 15.1) shows a very typical layout of an orchestra. There are 4 distinct groupings of instruments placed in arcs. The strings (violins, violas, cellos) are in the front, the woodwinds (flutes, clarinets, bassoons, oboes) in the middle, the brass (trumpets, French horns, trombones) in the back and the percussion (timpani, drums, xylophone, bells, gong) in the final layer.

Everyone is grouped so that they can work together as a sub-team, like instruments and instrument types near each other. These groupings are then situated so they can all function well together as an entire orchestra.

The like instruments will share music and listen to each other, working as one unified voice. The strings will synchronize their bow movements to create a more uniform sound. The percussionists need to move from instrument to instrument. Putting them in the back allows for that freedom of movement and positioning of each instrument so that those seated players will have a clear view of the conductor. The louder instruments are placed in the back to better assist with the balance of the volume carried out to the audience.

Each area has been positioned for its unique function – both working together and as a whole. Of course each individual instrument sounds beautiful alone and each group of instruments may sound wonderful together. The purpose and power of the orchestra is to work together, each performing their part to make the piece of music complete with the conductor providing the players with the overall interpretation of the music and keeping them working together harmoniously, all providing the audience with a satisfying end product.

How can you connect the design and function of the orchestra with how you might approach your business? What are the unique groups in your business and are they working together harmoniously? Do you have each group organized in a way that the entire team is contributing to the overall delight of your "audience"? How, as the leader, are you providing the guidance and structure to keep it functioning "harmoniously?"

Structure is an essential ingredient needed to allow your business to operate successfully and efficiently. Think of applying the idea of the structure of an orchestra to your business and see what breakthrough occurs for you and your team.

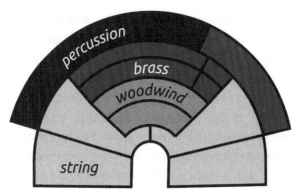

Figure 15.1 Orchestra Structure

The orchestra is a great structural model for business owners. Keeping order and harmony is an art that is influenced by form and function. The 9-Point System provides a structure with which to understand your business' form and function so you can create an organization that can operate effectively and be positioned to grow.

Integrating functional areas is critical to keep your organization from sliding into operating "silos " or "fiefdoms," working independently and, worse yet, as "enemies" of each other.

As a business owner, you are the leader of your company. It will be important for you to make sure that there is a continual integration and championing of all the people, processes, and

> *"Business process improvements have been responsible for reducing cost and cycle time by 90% and improving quality by 60%."* [1]

systems. You have the privilege and responsibility to set the tone and the standards for success, which includes redirecting and refocusing people when they deviate from those standards.

The underlying purpose of these distinct areas is to create order through a framework. This framework is primarily for you, as the business leader, to have a method to focus on discreet sections of the business for strategic thinking. It also creates a structure that creates teamwork, order, and organization for the functions that you will oversee.

Here is a visual of how all the parts of the 9-Point System work in continuity. Each area has unique functions while also supporting each other's goals, and the overall requirements and vision of the business owner.

Figure 15.2 Integrated Relationship: 9-Points

The critical component for successful integration is effective business owner leadership. The first step of providing clear, effective leadership is to take time to understand your organization, its strengths, weaknesses, and gaps. This 9-Point

System is designed to create a structure to look at your business in these discrete areas and begin to build the people, processes, and technology that will allow your business to create sustainable growth.

World Class Widget
- Learn how to build an effective team by accessing the **Building Blocks for Effective Teams.** For recording, worksheet, infographic, and blog go to: www.thestructuresolution.com

Parting Shots

The goal of this book has been to introduce you to a structure to help build and strengthen your business. The breakthrough results will come through applying the "rubber to the road" **Success Action** steps (found at the end of the chapters) to your business.

I belong to a group that is a collection of hard-working business professionals who all come together quarterly and operate as a Board of Directors to each other's businesses. One of the traditions at the end of each presentation is to provide "parting shots"[2]. It's short thought, point of emphasis, or overarching theme that has permeated the 2 – 3 hours of conversation. It is a nice way to end the meeting with recommendation and encouragement. I leave you too, with a parting shot that includes an example, a recommendation, and an encouragement for your success.

Structured for Success: A Bridge

Bridges are structures that get us across waterways, canyons, and other impassable areas. They are iconic representations of ingenuity and the ability of humans to accomplish incredible things. The structure of a bridge creates efficiency, allowing for shorter trips or using simpler transportation methods. They may be created through suspension only or by including supporting pillars. These are structures that allow more people to get to work, school, and travel spots that may not have been possible had there been no bridge.

The structure of a bridge alone is not fully functional until it has closed the gap, thus providing a method for getting people from one side to the other. Its purpose is to create a pathway across a gap.

Your company is in business, too, because it fills a unique gap in the marketplace. Your product or service provides a pathway for your customer's dilemma, problem, or needs to be solved. Without a structure to cross the gap, your business will be short-lived or highly chaotic, driven by whim rather than by design.

Just as a physical bridge takes someone from where they are to where they want to go, as a business owner, you have the opportunity to build bridges for your team, business, and customers. The gap may be skills for your team, revenues for your business, or the loyalty of your customers.

You may have discovered gaps in your business approach. You may have seen new ways you can approach your business to create more order and efficiency. As a perpetual learner, I find that I am always reading, thinking, testing, applying, and teaching. It's through these disciplines that I am able to continue to grow personally and professionally, providing more value to my business and to my clients.

It is my sincere desire that this book creates new and sustainable value for your business. I know it can with some intentional application and steps to action. Take advantage of the tools and templates I've posted as **World Class Widgets** and become a part of our Renaissance Works community through signing up for our Success Strategies (www.ren-works.com). I would love to hear about your insights and successes.

You have and create value for your team and customers. Go out and build the bridge that is **Structured for Success!**

Chapter 16. Next Steps: Becoming Structured for Success

"Failure is not fatal, but failure to change might be."
— John Wooden

If you have filled in the blanks in this book, then you are one step closer to achieving increased operational efficiency, for eliminating chaos and waste, and positioning your business for sustainable growth. If you have accessed the World Class

> **!** *"You are 33% more successful if you set and write down your goals and are accountable to others by sharing your progress on a regular basis."* [1]

Widgets and completed those, you have further invested in your progress. Setting up the preliminary structure of your business is a first and important step in being **Structured for Success**.

I invite you to leverage the following resources to keep your business on a pathway of growth (while also continually eliminating loss, rework, confusion, and stress).

My business, Renaissance Works, is always focused on making things happen and we want to see higher levels of success happen for you as well. This world needs greater leadership and excellence and a business owner — like you — can have a huge influence. You have the power to make a difference for you, your family, those you hire and the community you serve. We would love to be a part of supporting your success.

Here are some additional resources that are available from Renaissance Works:

- **Success Strategies Series**: Recordings & written notes on topics useful for addressing your operational issues.

- **Functional Strategy Session**: 90-minute live consulting and coaching session designed to map out your functional structure and determine transition and action plans to support your specific 3 to 6-month and 6 to12-month business objectives.

- **Business Board**: 6-month program, which includes personal coaching and group discussions, facilitated by a master business coach. The problem solving and accountability will propel your business forward. Like-minded business people join in confidential and supportive businesses conversations.

Contact us: success@ren-works.com

Footnotes

Chapter 1:   1 - The 2009 Shift Index, Industry metrics and
               perspectives, Deloitte Center for the Edge,
               2009.

Chapter 3:   1 - High-Rise Security and Fire Life Safety, 3rd
               Edition Geoff Craighead Butterworth-Heinemann

Chapter 4:   1- The history of department stores:
               www.departmentstorehistory.net

               2 - KPMG, Confronting complexity, January 2011.

Chapter 5:   1 - The Staggering Cost of Mis-Hires, Article
               #107, Positioning Systems, July 27, 2010

               2- Studies Show IT Projects Experience High
               Failure Rates, Wiley, July 2010

Chapter 9:   1 - ISR employee engagement report, IRS, 2006;
               The Economics of Engagement, Human Capital
               Institute, 2009; Engagement inspiration at
               manager communications conference, March
               2011.

Chapter 10:   1 - Clear Direction in a Complex World, 2011-
               2012 Change and Communication ROI Study
               Report, Towers Watson.

Chapter 11:   1 - Companies Want Better Data Analysis For
               Decision-Making In New Wave Of Technology
               Upgrades, Says KPMG Survey KPMG, December,
               2011

Chapter 12:   1- Keith Cunningham frequently reminds business owners about the distinction between delegation and abdication which is where I first heard of this concept.

Chapter 13:   1- "Employee Attitude" Survey, Cornerstone On Demand, March 2010.

Chapter 14:   1 - American Institute of Stress, NIOSH report, CDC Publications Number 99-101 accessed December, 2011

2 - This quote has been attribute to a number of sources including most prominently, James Drucker. However, I found it interesting to see a possible first connection to this idea from the Scottish physicist, Lord Kelvin. According to the *Encyclopaedia of Occupational Health and Safety*, by Jeanne Mager Stellman (page 1992), Kelvin said in his May 3, 1883, lecture on "Electrical Units of Measurement" (*Popular Lectures*, Vol. 1, page 73): *"I often say that when you can measure what you are speaking about, and express it in numbers, you know something about it; but when you cannot express it in numbers, your knowledge is of a meagre and unsatisfactory kind; it may be the beginning of knowledge, but you have scarcely, in your thoughts, advanced to the stage of science, whatever the matter may be."*

Chapter 15:   1 - "Business Process Management's Success Hinges on Business-Led Initiatives," Gartner; Building the Business Case for BPM, Oracle Corp, March 2009

2 - Keith Cunningham created this as part of his Board of Directors program (www.keystothevault.com).

Chapter 16:   1 - a) Can use "Change Anything: The New Science of Personal Success" by Kerry Patterson; b) Also refer to: http://www.dominican.edu/dominicannews/study-backs-up-strategies-for-achieving-goals. Dr. Gail Matthews confirms the unconnected "1953 Yale Study of Goals."

About Karen Logan

Karen Logan is CEO and Managing Partner of Renaissance Works, Inc. For the past 20 years she has helped Business Owners and Fortune 500 companies build efficiency and productivity into their businesses, reducing waste and increasing peace of mind. She has a natural ability to create order out chaos and to break out the complex into the simple.

She loves providing a pathway of growth for business owners by taking best practices of the Corporate world to the business owner in a simple and scalable method that creates order and efficiency for the owner and their teams. She has found that many business owners are great at what they do, but need significant help to grow their business and breakthrough to the next level of income.

She also has become an avid runner over the years. Keeping healthy in body and mind has been an essential ingredient in serving her clients as well as teaching others to succeed at the intellectual sport called business.

Her mission is to help business owners to increase their success through applying order and structure to their business operations. Come and join the movement to be **Structured for Success**: www.ren-works.com.

CPSIA information can be obtained at www.ICGtesting.com
Printed in the USA
LVOW01s2307230714

395702LV00022B/1722/P